Debrett's Guide to
Civilised Separation

WITH MISHCON DE REYA

Debrett's Guide to Civilised Separation
in association with Mishcon de Reya

Published by Debrett's Limited
18-20 Hill Rise
Richmond
Surrey TW10 6UA

www.debretts.com
www.mishcon.com

Concept and writing
Elizabeth Wyse

Design
Karen Wilks

Illustrations
Zoe More O'Ferrall

Editorial Director, Mishcon de Reya
Miles Geffin

ISBN 978-1-870-520-997

Printed and bound by push-print.com

Introduction

Relationship breakdown affects countless numbers of people each year. The combination of stress and emotional and financial upheaval can be overwhelming.

Debrett's, Britain's leading experts on manners and behaviour, has been an authoritative social commentator since 1789. Debrett's has always emphasised that manners help to make the world a calm, comfortable and civilised place. Even in the most difficult of personal situations, courteous and considerate behaviour can help to reduce unnecessary animosity and distress.

Founded in 1937, Mishcon de Reya is a law firm with offices in London and New York offering a wide range of legal services to companies and individuals. The lawyers in the Firm's highly-regarded family department have acted in some of the most high profile and important cases in recent years. Recognising the importance of civility in separation proceedings, in 2009 the Firm lobbied Government for the introduction of national 'Conflict Clinics' as an alternative to the financial and emotional cost of family litigation.

Debrett's has worked with Mishcon de Reya to produce this guide in order to dispel common myths surrounding separation and to provide information and reassurance for those who need it.

Contents

"To love and win is the best thing.
To love and lose, the next best."

William M. Thackeray

What is a Marriage?

"Marriage is an alliance entered into by a man who can't sleep with the window shut, and a woman who can't sleep with the window open."

George Bernard Shaw

A History of Marriage

In the 13th century, the Church in England confirmed that the free consent of both spouses, not formal religious solemnities, was the essence of a valid marriage. Many people chose to make these vows in church.

But the situation became increasingly ambiguous, with many people living together in a number of different circumstances, and no legal consensus about what constituted a legally binding marriage. When the State started taxing marriage in the 1690s an increasing number of people settled for informal unions. Couples considered themselves 'married in the sight of God' and that was sufficient.

A public ceremony in a church served the function of openly proclaiming the marriage's validity. But clergymen also conducted clandestine marriages, without the reading of the banns or the issuing of a valid licence, and these were increasingly popular. Clandestine marriages generated many abuses; heiresses were kidnapped, drugged and forcibly married, and there was a large number of incestuous, bigamous and under-age unions.

In 1753 Lord Hardwicke's Marriage Act stipulated that marriages should be performed by ordained Anglican clergymen in church premises, after thrice-called banns or purchase of a licence from a bishop.

The Act applied to England only and some couples evaded the restrictions by travelling to various Scottish border villages in order to marry. In the 1770s a toll road was constructed, passing through the Borders village of Gretna Green, which became synonymous with runaway weddings.

One in six couples in Britain live together without getting married.

** *From 1696 it was possible to get married without banns or a special licence within the Liberty of the Fleet Debtors' Prison. This included the pubs and inns, which specialised in inexpensive services. By the 1740s more than half of all London weddings were celebrated within the Fleet's boundaries. In 1753, more stringent criteria ensured Fleet marriages were no longer legal.*

"Life isn't a matter of milestones but of moments."
Rose F. Kennedy

MARRIAGE MILESTONES

1753: The Marriage Act, described as 'An Act for the Better Preventing of Clandestine Marriage', is introduced, requiring a formal ceremony in order to enter a valid marriage.

1870: The Married Women's Property Act entitles wives to both own any money they earn and to inherit property.

1882: The Married Women's Property Act gives statutory recognition to a wife's right to own, buy and sell her separate property. A husband and wife are now two separate legal entities, each able to sue, be sued, contract debt and be made bankrupt. The wife's property is no longer surrendered to her husband on marriage.

In English law matrimony is the estate a man and woman enter when they consent and contract to co-habit with each other and each other only.

Permissible Marriages

A man and woman may marry if they're aged 16 or over (though parental consent is required for people aged 16 or 17) and if they are free to marry (single, widowed, divorced or previously in a dissolved civil partnership). Restrictions relating to consanguinity apply, preventing marriages between couples with a close genetic relationship, or with adoptive parents or adopted children.

Civil Partnerships

The Civil Partnership Act of 2004 allows same-sex couples to enter into a civil partnership, which offers identical practical legal rights and responsibilities to marriage. They are not available to different-sex couples.

Overseas Marriages

The law of the country in which the marriage was contracted governs the formal validity of the marriage, and the UK courts will recognise overseas marriages that are formalised according to local law.

Co-Habiting Couples

There is a persistent myth that 'a common law' husband or wife is legally protected on separation, but in reality there is no such thing as a common law husband or wife, and many non-married couples are therefore not legally protected. To avoid unjust conditions on separation, especially where children are involved, co-habiting couples are advised to enter into a cohabitation agreement.

What is a Divorce?

"Divorce is probably of nearly the same date as marriage. I believe, however, that marriage is some weeks the more ancient."

Voltaire

A History of Divorce

Before the Reformation in England marriage was governed by Canon law and could not be dissolved. Most people tended to simply desert each other if their marriage failed.

Judicial separation, overseen by the ecclesiastical courts, could be used by wives to improve the financial terms of an existing separation, or by husbands to avoid paying alimony to an adulterous wife. A judicial separation became one of the essential steps in obtaining a parliamentary divorce, a very rare full divorce with right to remarry, granted to an individual by an Act of Parliament as an exception to the rule of the indissolubility of marriage. The other, necessary step was the suit for criminal conversation, or 'crim. con.', a civil suit for monetary damages brought by a cuckolded husband against a wife's lover.

Divorce Law Reform

In 1857 an Act of Parliament introduced the possibility of divorce being granted in a civil court in England and Wales. From 1857 to 1922, adultery was effectively considered the sole ground for divorce, although a husband's adultery had to be accompanied by one or more other specified matrimonial transgressions – incest, cruelty, bigamy, sodomy or desertion. The same restrictions did not apply to husbands who petitioned for divorce because of their wives' adultery. It was only in 1923 that these conditions imposed on petitioning wives were abolished.

In 1938 an Act of Parliament extended the grounds on which divorce was admissible to include desertion, cruelty and insanity.

The 1969 Divorce Reform Act, consolidated into the 1973 Matrimonial Causes Act,

In 1911 there were 580 divorces, in 1947 there were 60,000, in 2009 there were 126,596.

** A decree of Judicial Separation brings to an end all marital obligations. This decree may be sought if one of the parties is opposed to divorce (normally for religious reasons), if the separation is required during the first year of the marriage, or if there are difficulties in proving the irretrievable breakdown of marriage.

introduced a solitary ground for divorce: 'the irretrievable breakdown of marriage', to be proved by one or more of five 'facts' (adultery, behaviour, desertion, two years' separation with respondent's consent to divorce, five years' separation). Divorce could only be petitioned after three years of marriage, unless there were exceptional circumstances.

In 1984 the Matrimonial and Family Proceedings Act introduced an absolute time bar before a divorce petition could be sought (one year after the date of marriage).

Annulment of Marriage

An annulment, unlike a divorce, is a judicial statement that there was never a marriage.

A marriage may be annulled on the grounds that it is 'void' for a number of reasons: if either party is under 16, if the parties were within the prohibited degrees of relationship, if the marriage was bigamous, or if the parties were not respectively male and female. A marriage may be annulled on the grounds that it is 'voidable' if there is evidence of the following: non-consummation (owing either to incapacity or refusal); non-consent to the marriage on the grounds of duress, mistake or unsound mind; mental disorder; one of the parties was suffering from a communicable venereal disease; the woman was pregnant with another partner's child at the time of marriage; change of gender issues.

The Role of Adultery

Adultery remained the sole ground for divorce for both parties until 1938, when cruelty, desertion and insanity were also recognised. Much of the stigma, scandal and scaremongering that surrounded the question of divorce emanated from this focus on adultery, and the humiliating need to prove, to the courts' satisfaction, that it had actually taken place.

HOLY DEADLOCK

In 1934, A. P. Herbert, a professional humorist who wrote for *Punch* magazine, wrote the definitive divorce novel, *Holy Deadlock*. When his protagonist hires a co-respondent to enact a fake adultery in a Brighton hotel, his choice of the sleazy seaside town is his downfall, arousing the Judge's suspicions – "A hotel? At Brighton?...All this seems very familiar." The petition is dismissed. A. P. Herbert went on to become an Independent MP for Oxford University in 1935 and campaigned for reform of the divorce laws. The result was the passing of the Matrimonial Causes Act in 1938, which extended the grounds on which divorce was admissible, to include desertion, cruelty and insanity as well as adultery.

The Burden of Proof

It is very rare for adulterous couples to be surprised mid-act. Judges agreed that, from time to time, there were 'cases in which passion amounting to insanity may lead a person to forget all sense of duty, all regard for decency and all fear of detection', but in general they were of the opinion that adultery necessitated discretion and that detection was actively avoided.

Even when the services of a private detective were enlisted, judges were inclined to dismiss their testimony on the grounds that they were motivated by pecuniary self-interest to find evidence of adultery.

In reality, if a couple behaved with an adulterous inclination, for example if they were seen behaving with 'indecent familiarity', the court believed that adultery could be inferred. A barman who testified that he had seen his wife kissing the co-respondent, and had seen her sitting in a room with the co-respondent in her underwear, was granted a decree on the grounds that his wife had committed adultery.

The 'Hotel Divorce'

From the inception of the 1857 Divorce Act the vast majority of divorces were undefended, and both husbands and wives were anxious to bring their marriage to an end. To bring this about, the practice developed of one side

"Where there's Marriage without Love, there will always be Love without Marriage."
Benjamin Franklin

*** Before 1858, true divorce, freeing both partners to re-marry, was by an
Act of Parliament and was rare and expensive. It protected the husband's
property from being inherited by the spurious issue of an adulterous wife.
Under 300 such divorces were granted, only four of the petitioners were
women who, besides alleging adultery, had to prove life-threatening cruelty.*

THE LEGAL PROCESS

providing the other with a confession that he/
she had committed adultery (until 1923 it was
a more straightforward matter to prove the
wife's adultery, as there was no need to give
proof of one of the extra offences of incest,
bigamy, cruelty, sodomy, and desertion that
were required in the case of husbands).

To prove adultery to the satisfaction of
the courts a couple were obliged to provide
evidence, such as hotel bills. By the 1930s it
had become common practice for couples to
provide sham proof of adultery by staying in
a hotel (Brighton was a favourite choice) with
a paid 'co-respondent'. Evidence of this false
adultery was obtained by a private detective
(photographs, bills, witness testimony) and
duly presented to the courts. The practice
was widely pilloried, and became the subject
of many satirical attacks, including Evelyn
Waugh's *A Handful of Dust* (1934).

In 1973, new legislation was introduced
which revolutionised the process of divorce;
public hearings were rare and obtaining
a divorce became a form-filling exercise.
Adultery became one of the five 'facts'
supporting a petition for divorce and the
central role it had played in court proceedings
was quickly diminished.

Today, the presence of adultery in the
breakdown of a relationship has no bearing
on any financial settlement or the care
arrangements for children of the family.

Legal Issues

Do you need a Lawyer?

Before you reach any final decision about bringing your marriage to an end, it is a good idea to seek joint counselling from an organisation such as Relate. A counsellor will offer you a calm, civilised and impartial environment in which you can safely explore your feelings about the relationship before you make an absolute decision.

If you do decide to separate or divorce, then you should seek legal advice. A specialist family lawyer can explain the legal issues that arise from relationship breakdown so that you understand fully the options open to you – you can then decide how you wish to proceed.

In addition to advising on the dissolution of the marriage itself, a lawyer can also advise you on the various different options regarding the care arrangements for any children and on the financial issues that arise on divorce.

A specialist lawyer can also advise you on the various alternatives to resolve any disputes. Litigation should be the last, not the first, option and good lawyers will discuss various alternatives such as mediation and family therapy. They may recommend collaborative law, when lawyers representing each side meet (with their clients) and negotiate.

Mediation

Since 6 April 2011, anyone wanting to use the courts to resolve a legal dispute over childcare arrangements or matrimonial finances will have to undergo a compulsory mediation assessment session first (although couples retain the right to insist on going to court).

In the financial year 2007/08 the Law Services Commisssion spent £150m on private family proceedings – only £13m of this was spent on mediation.

** Since 2009 six out of ten legally aided divorce cases, where couples seeking divorce are legally enforced to consider mediation, are being settled out of court.

However, cases that involve domestic violence or child protection issues will generally still bypass mediation and go straight to court.

If any disagreements between separating partners have been resolved, the lawyer will be able to draw up the documents necessary for any financial agreement to be binding. If disagreements cannot be resolved through negotiation or other means of alternative dispute resolution then a lawyer can guide you through the process of family litigation.

The Legal Pathway

There is no legal requirement that you retain a lawyer to represent or assist you in divorce proceedings.

There are many resources available on and off line to enable you to obtain the forms necessary for you to obtain your own divorce and/or to obtain information about the divorce process and how to resolve issues arising from relationship breakdown.

However, the law is complex and it can be a false economy not to take legal advice. A lawyer can help you deal with the legal issues surrounding your divorce, issues you might miss if you tried a do-it-yourself divorce. In most cases there will be financial issues that need to be resolved. Where there are issues over the childcare arrangements it is particularly important to obtain legal advice.

HOW TO CHOOSE A LAWYER CHECKLIST

⇆ Have you spoken to friends, family and colleagues about their experiences? Word-of-mouth may be a good indicator.

⇆ Is your lawyer experienced in family law?

⇆ Do you have a good rapport?

⇆ Are the lawyer's fees acceptable?

⇆ Is your lawyer a registered specialist with the Law Society, Resolution or the International Academy of Matrimonial Lawyers (if there are cross border issues)?

⇆ Is there good chemistry? Divorce and associated proceedings can take some time to resolve and developing a relationship with your lawyer will assist.

⇆ Mediation and conflict resolution are particularly good at minimising the detrimental impact of divorce on children. Is your lawyer a trained mediator? If not, is he/she open to this approach?

"All government, indeed every human benefit and enjoyment, every virtue, and every prudent act, is founded on compromise and barter."
Edmund Burke

Getting the Most From Your Lawyer

"The leading rule for the lawyer, as for the man of every other calling, is diligence. Leave nothing for tomorrow which can be done today."

Abraham Lincoln

Be candid. Generally, everything you tell your lawyer is confidential. Your lawyer cannot properly advise or represent you unless he or she is aware of all the facts.

Listen to your lawyer. Even if it's advice or information you don't want to hear, your lawyer knows the law and how it's likely to be applied to your facts and your case. Take a notebook to legal consultations and make notes of important points, or questions you'd like to come back to. If you act in a businesslike way you will feel more on top of the situation, and less victimised.

Make lists. Before seeing your lawyer make a list of everything you want to discuss – that way you'll feel more in control, and you can ensure that precious time isn't wasted…

Answer questions directly. Your lawyer needs detailed information and direct answers to questions to best help you.

Ask questions. You need to understand how the law applies in your particular case and understand what your lawyer is telling you. You also need to know what you and your lawyer are going to do next.

Keep careful records. Documents, letters, bank statements, financial documents and receipts are likely to be very important to your lawyer. Try and get on top of your family's finances, and don't let your partner bully you.

Trust your lawyer. You and your lawyer need to work together as a team.

"Compromise is the best and cheapest lawyer."
Robert Louis Stevenson

** *The average cost of a divorce in the UK is £13,000.*

Provide information and documents. If your lawyer asks you to provide a document or information, it is likely to be important. Getting the right information to your lawyer will expedite the process and save on costs.

Return telephone calls and emails from your lawyer. Your lawyer should make every effort to respond to you in a timely fashion – you should reciprocate.

Be realistic about what you want. It's no good claiming a Fortnum & Mason's lifestyle, when you've always been satisfied with Sainsbury's. Most legal disputes end in a settlement. Although you may not get everything you want, neither will your spouse.

Be flexible. There are many ways to get what you want from a case. Be willing to give up what's less important so you can get what's most important.

Follow your lawyer's advice. Unless you follow your lawyer's advice, you won't get the best possible legal help.

Don't use your lawyer as a counsellor. It's tempting to confide in a sympathetic lawyer, but it's foolish to do so while the meter is ticking away. Seek counselling from professionals, or confide in close friends.

Don't Be Scared
Legal letters are designed to be threatening, so don't get into a panic if the letters from your spouse's lawyers seem overbearing. Just make sure you furnish your own lawyer with any information that has been requested, and leave them to deal with the legal jargon. That's what you're paying for.

Don't Be Vindictive
Throwing your husband's vintage wine collection down the loo or cutting his suits to shreds might seem like a therapeutic gesture when you're in the throes of rage and despair, but it can rebound on you and undermine your case. Judges will take a dim view of vindictive behaviour, so it's far better to hold your head up high and retain the civilised high ground.

Don't Waste Your Lawyer's Time
Arguing about which party should have the cream sofa or best dinner service is not a good use of your lawyer's time or fees. As much as possible, you should try to resolve these issues with your spouse. If you are already separated, you might be able to divide these items by agreement (perhaps with the help of friends, or even a counsellor) before the case has been completed. It's foolish to run up substantial fees arguing about items that have modest cash value.

Children

"There is frequently more to be learned from the unexpected questions of a child than the discourses of men."

John Locke

In all matters relating to children, the child's welfare is the main concern of the Court. The Court will have to take a number of factors into consideration when making decisions about a child's future, and the Children's Act (1989) has sought to create a flexible system that allows the Court a wide range of options. The Court is responsible both for setting up the arrangements for the child's future life, and in monitoring and resolving disputes between parents about those arrangements.

Putting Children First

The Court must address the following:

⇆ The wishes and feelings of the child.

⇆ The needs of the child (physical, emotional and educational).

⇆ The age, sex and background of the child.

⇆ The likely effect on the child of a change of circumstance.

⇆ Any harm the child has suffered or is at risk of suffering.

⇆ The capabilities of each of his/her parents, or anyone else concerned, to meet his/her emotional, physical and educational needs.

Once the Court has made its assessment of the family and its situation, it can make the following two orders:

Residence Order

This Order settles the arrangements relating to where the child lives, and with whom. The Order is made in relation to one of the parents, and confers parental responsibility on that person. If a Residence Order is put in place, the child cannot be removed from the

"The separated parent's role in the lives of his or her children retains the same degree of importance as when the parents were living together."
Sir Nicholas Wall, President of the Family Division of the High Court

** *The Custody of Infants Act of 1839 permitted a mother to petition the courts for custody of her children up to the age of seven, and for access in respect of older children. Until then, fathers had automatically been awarded custody of the children, regardless of the reasons for the divorce.*

UK without the written consent of everyone who has parental responsibility or the leave of the Court.

Contact Order

This Order requires the person with whom the child lives (the residential parent) to allow the child to visit, or stay with, or have other contact with the person named in the Order.

If there are disagreements between separating parents over various issues – for example the school the child is to attend, or the religion he/she is to follow – then the Court can make a Specific Issue Order, giving directions. A Prohibited Steps Order indicates that certain specific steps cannot be taken without the permission of the Court.

Relocation

If the primary (residential) carer decides to move within the UK this can have a negative impact on the other parent's contact with the child, and the plan to relocate can therefore be challenged in Court and be made subject to a Prohibited Steps Order.

Money Matters

"When it is a question of money, everybody is of the same religion."

Voltaire

A pension fund can form the largest capital part of a settlement, particularly when there has been a long marriage.

When it comes to distributing financial assets one of the main considerations of the Court is the welfare of any child who is under the age of eighteen.

The matrimonial home is always considered a matrimonial asset, even if it was owned solely by one partner before the marriage, and is therefore subject to equal division.

If an equal division of all the other assets of the marriage results in both parties having enough to meet their own needs, and those of the children, then matters will be resolved.

If the division of capital does not meet the needs of one party, or if one partner has suffered an economic disadvantage because of the marriage (for example giving up work to look after the children), then the Court may order an unequal distribution of capital.

** A landmark case, White v White, 1996. Martin White and his wife Pamela, married for 33 years, had run a farming business, worth about £4m. At first Pamela White was awarded £980,000, but she took the case to the court of appeal, then the House of Lords in 2000, and was finally awarded £1.7m in recognition of her contribution as a 'homemaker'.

Conversely, if one partner has generated significant matrimonial assets, then the Court may choose to award the receiving party less than half the total assets to reflect this.

Factors for Consideration

⇆ The income, earning capacity, property of each partner, and any potential for an increase in earning capacity
⇆ The financial needs, obligations and responsibilities of each partner
⇆ The family's standard of living before the breakdown
⇆ The age of the couple, and the duration of their marriage
⇆ Any physical or mental disability
⇆ The contributions made by each partner to the welfare of the family, for example, looking after the home, childcare
⇆ The conduct of each party
⇆ The value of any benefits (such as a spouse's pension) that may be lost following a divorce.

A Clean Break?

If there is not enough capital to ensure that both parties' needs are adequately met, then the Court may have to order that ongoing maintenance is paid by one party to the other. An order of maintenance is generally only terminated by the re-marriage of the partner who is receiving it, or by death, or by a further Court Order.

The Court assesses maintenance by taking a number of factors into consideration: the financial needs of the ex-spouse, an evaluation of the standard of living the couple enjoyed before the divorce, and an assessment of the paying partner's ability to meet these financial demands. If the paying partner has a high income, then the Court will tend to be generous in the assessment of the other partner's needs.

SEPARATION FROM BED AND BOARD

Before the Divorce Reform Act of 1857 many unhappy couples had recourse to the ecclesiastical court of Doctors' Commons to obtain a legal separation from 'bed and board'. The former husband and wife were separated, but were not entitled to find new spouses: a wife who was unable to remarry could easily fall into penury. If the cuckolded husband was intent on revenge he could bring a case of 'criminal conversation' (adultery) against his wife's lover. The law accepted that the wife was one of her husband's possessions. Therefore, if someone else had slept with her, thus defiling his property, he was entitled to seek compensation.

Court Proceedings

"Those who expect moments of change to be comfortable and free of conflict have not learned their history."

John Wallach Scott

Preparing for Court

You will be examined and cross-examined on the basis of what is written in your witness statement(s). Ensure that you have read and re-read your witness statement and if you are unsure about anything in your statement, or realise that something – however insignificant – is incorrect, ask your solicitor.

Read the other party's statement carefully. Issues may have arisen since you signed your witness statement. Ensure you know of these. Make sure that you have considered these points in line with what you wrote in your witness statement.

Your solicitor may provide you with other documents in preparation for trial, for example counsel's skeleton argument. Read these documents carefully and if anything is not clear ask your solicitor.

In Court

You will be asked to confirm your religion for the purposes of swearing an appropriate oath.

Your barrister will ask you to turn to your witness statement(s) in the bundle(s) in front of you. You will be asked to confirm that it is your signature on it/them. Your witness statement(s) automatically become your evidence in chief. You do not need to repeat what you have already said in them.

Your barrister may take you through questions relating to matters that have arisen since you signed your statement, or he may 'amplify' what you have said in your statement, before you are cross-examined.

If your barrister has not gone through the evidence set out in your witness statement it does not mean that the judge has not taken it into account.

** Only Justices of the Supreme Court or Justices sitting in the Court of Appeal are addressed as 'My Lord' or 'My Lady'. Circuit judges are called 'Your Honour', while District Judges and Magistrates are referred to as 'Sir' or 'Madam'.

DO'S AND DON'TS IN COURT

Do Dress Smartly...
Dress smartly, but not ostentatiously and ensure that you feel comfortable in whatever you're wearing.

Maintain eye contact...
Look the judge in the face, sit up straight and speak loudly and clearly.

Direct your answers to the judge...
Address the judge, whoever is asking you the questions. If you don't understand the question ask for it to be repeated or rephrased.

Slow down...
Remember the judge is taking notes on your answers, so watch out for his pen.

Just ask...
If you want a break ask for one. If you need time to compose yourself, ask for it.

Explain...
If you can't remember specifics, say so.

Be Amenable...
Never question the relevance of the question being put to you.

Don't mutter or mumble...
And avoid speaking when you've not been spoken to or slumping in your seat.

Avoid arguing...
Don't argue with the judge or the counsel. If you disagree just say so. You are paying your counsel to make your arguments for you in court.

Don't get personal...
Even if you think another witness has been untruthful, you don't need to call them a liar. Just state your disagreement.

Don't be aggressive...
You may find that the barrister questioning you is confrontational, but don't rise to it.

Curb your Suspicions...
Not everything you're asked is intended to catch you out; some questions may be completely straightforward.

Don't worry about hindsight...
If you are asked why you didn't take another course of action that you didn't think of at the time, admit that you didn't think of it.

COURT STRUCTURE

Supreme Court
Final Court of Appeal in the UK. Hears appeals on points of law in cases of major importance from the Court of Appeal (and in some limited cases from the High Court).

Court of Appeal
Hears appeals from the High Court on points of law.

High Court
Hears complex cases and also appeals from County Courts.

County Court
Hears a wide range of family cases.

Magistrates' Court
Hears a range of family proceedings, including those in relation to children's issues

Spreading the News

"Bad news isn't wine.
It doesn't improve with age."

Colin Powell

Telling friends and family about an imminent divorce is not a pleasant task, but it is vital that you ensure the news is disseminated as quickly as possible. Procrastination will just mean that people find out the wrong way. Your marriage break-up will be the gossip of your social circle, and people who are close to you will feel, justifiably, that they have been marginalised.

Children should be the first to hear about a divorce, and explaining such a momentous event must be very sensitively handled. Always break the news to the children with your partner in private, and ensure that you display a united front. Explain that the divorce has nothing to do with them and reassure them that you still love them.

Be prepared; your children are likely to bombard you with questions about who will live where, if and when they'll see a departing parent, who'll keep the pets, whether they'll have to move house or change schools. Things will go much better if you have detailed answers to these questions ready.

Stand by your Decision

Be prepared for disbelief, anger, incredulity. Friends may protest that you had an excellent marriage – but remember that nobody really has an insight into the workings of a marriage apart from the two protagonists.

If you feel beleaguered by your friends' reaction, it isn't rude to say " I really don't want to talk about this – I've made my decision." As you move on, you may feel more open to discussion.

The median duration of marriage for divorces granted in 2009 was 11.4 years.

** It has been predicted that 45% of all marriages in England and Wales will end in divorce if 2005 rates continue. However in 2009, the divorce rate in England and Wales fell to 10.5 divorcing people per 1,000 married population compared with the 2005 figure of 14.1. The divorce rate in 2009 was at its lowest level since 1977 when it was 10.3.

"The discipline of the written word punishes both stupidity and dishonesty."
John Steinbeck

Communicating Effectively

Once you have told your children it is vital that you tell your immediate family circle – you wouldn't want grandparents to hear about your divorce from the children.

⇆ As with all bad news, text messaging is inappropriate. Ideally, you will talk to close friends and family face-to-face.

⇆ If this is impossible, then consider writing a handwritten letter. You will want to explain your decision, but avoid vitriol and recriminations – intemperate remarks, in writing, may come back to haunt you.

⇆ State clearly that the divorce is a difficult decision and a last resort, and stress that every possible effort has been made to save the marriage (this may pre-empt well-meaning attempts to persuade you to try again).

⇆ If you don't feel that the formality of the written word is for you, a telephone call may be acceptable. Emails are a casual form of communication, and are not appropriate for big news, or for close relatives.

⇆ Take the time to explain the situation, either in person or in writing, to your children's school and teachers.

Divorce and Children

Children crave continuity, and it is up to the divorcing parents to provide that. Changes to your children's life should be introduced slowly and sensitively – if you manage this process effectively, they will see new doors opening.

Two Homes

Do your utmost to ensure that each parent provides a comfortable and welcoming home base for the children. Ensure that the children have their own room/s (no sleeping on sofa-beds), which they can arrange, and personalise, as they choose. They will need a place to store their possessions.

If you are the parent that is setting up a new home, try and avoid the temptation to out-do the children's experience and expectations. Packing their rooms with flat-screen tvs, state-of-the-art games consoles and the latest computer equipment, when they are used to more spartan facilities, is a blatant attempt to curry favour. You will not only antagonise your ex-partner, you will unsettle the children and may make them feel dissatisfied with their old home. They will be much more contented if their two homes are not poles apart.

If, on the other hand, your circumstances are making austerity imperative, don't apologise. Children will enjoy improvising and making do if you turn it into an adventure.

*** Just under half of couples divorcing in 2009 had at least one child aged under 16 – there were 99,543 children aged under 16 who were in families where the parents divorced in England and Wales. Of these 21% of children were under five and 63% under 11.*

Do's and Don'ts

⇆ Protect your children

Face-to-face arguments and angry telephone calls should always be conducted behind closed doors.

⇆ Don't confide in your children

They lack the maturity or the objectivity to understand and will find your distress frightening. They may convey a garbled version of your confidences to your ex-partner.

⇆ Never use children as go-betweens

Children are not effective messengers and misunderstandings will ensue. You may also be revealing a range of anarchic emotions to your children which they are unable to assimilate.

⇆ Don't question your children

Don't cross-examine your children about your ex. They have had to redefine their relationship with both parents and will resent your attempts to invade that territory.

⇆ Do remain unfailingly polite

Biting back bitter remarks and keeping cool will make everyone more calm and relaxed.

⇆ Conduct handovers with dignity

Find a quiet, private place, and avoid noisy cafés, shopping malls and petrol stations.

Cooperating With Courtesy

"Courage is what it takes to stand up and speak; courage is also what it takes to sit down and listen."

Winston Churchill

If you're newly divorced, with children, it is imperative that you and your ex-partner work together. This is a long-term commitment and it is important that you start off as you mean to go on.

New Roles

Don't allow roles to become polarised. If one parent is entirely responsible for the mundanities of everyday life (laundry, shopping, school, homework) and the other sweeps the children off their feet every weekend for a round of treats, outings and parental indulgence, you will be creating a regrettable precedent. The children will alternate between dissatisfaction and over-stimulation, and eventually will become very unhappy. The downtrodden parent will be understandably resentful.

Ensure that each parent takes his/her share of the practicalities. This might mean, for example, that the non-residential parent makes a commitment to oversee the children's homework each week.

Remember, your new life as divorced parents is really not about scoring points off each other, but ensuring that your children's life is stable, secure and contented.

Avoid Competing

Trying to buy your children's love and loyalty is ultimately fruitless. You will find yourself quickly spiralling into a frenzy of competitive gift giving, expensive treats, ever-more-exotic holidays, designer labels. At worst, your children will become spoilt and over-indulged, adept at playing you off against each other.

** Since 1998 the average age at divorce in England and Wales has risen from 40.4 to 44.0 years for men and from 37.9 to 41.5 years for women, partly reflecting the rise in age at marriage.

"Life is short but there is always time for courtesy."
Ralph Waldo Emerson

GOLDEN RULES

Communicate...
Discuss all aspects of your children's life – their friends, social life, schoolwork – with your ex-partner. You could arrange to have a regular phone conversation.

Correspond...
If phone or face-to-face conversations are quick to ignite into rage and recrimination, email regularly, and keep the correspondence focused and businesslike.

Share...
Keeping important information to yourself will not give you power, it will simply jeopardise your children's happiness.

Consult...
When you have to make important decisions concerning your children's life, make it clear to them that you will need to consult your ex-partner. They will see that you are treating each other with respect.

Liaise...
Agree spending limits at Christmas and birthdays, and cooperate over big decisions (mobile phones, games consoles etc).

Explain...
For your children's sake, you and your ex-partner must ensure that everyone is informed about your separation. Write the school a note to explain the situation, and outline any practical consequences – changes in picking up from school arrangements, or a request for communications to be made to both parents, for example.

Inform...
Ensure that the parents of your children's friends are also informed. If they are aware of your situation, they may be able to offer extra help and support (sleepovers, play dates etc.). They will also be able to avoid asking your children tactless questions, and can explain the situation to their own children.

Agree...
To avoid complete confusion, you should agree on responsibilities for specific tasks with your ex-partner at the outset. These might include taking the children to the hairdresser or dentist, buying school uniforms, dealing with the family doctor.

Mementoes

"I've given my memoirs far more thought than any of my marriages. You can't divorce a book."

Gloria Swanson

The big decisions about the division of your assets have already been made. But what about the flotsam and jetsam, often accumulated over many years of married life? Ensuring that your joint possessions are fairly distributed will demand reserves of tact and diplomacy.

Photographs

This is an emotive area, as it touches poignantly on shared memories. The important thing to remember is that, while you may utterly reject these painful reminders of your wedding day or your years together as young parents, or indeed feel possessive of them, these images are an important part of your children's history, and may also be valued by other family members. So be prepared to relinquish control over them.

These days, most photography is digital, which makes it straightforward to duplicate photos many times. Even if you were the main photographer in the family, it is unfair to lay a personal claim to family photographs. Simply create a set of DVDs of duplicate images and hand them over to your ex-partner. It is then his/her responsibility to distribute photos to other family members.

Possessions pre-dating Marriage

In most circumstances, these will not be considered assets of the marriage; they are your own possessions, and should not form part of the divorce settlement.

Engagement Rings

The engagement ring is an outright gift given to the woman on the condition of marriage,

"The photograph is concerned with the power that the past has to interfere with the present: the time bomb in the cupboard."
Penelope Lively

** In 2006 divorcing insurance magnate John Charman was ordered to pay his wife £48m, reducing his total assets to £87m. It is thought to be the largest divorce settlement in British legal history.

and having met that condition, she is entitled to keep it even after the marriage's dissolution. If the ring is a precious heirloom, handed down on the paternal side, returning it is entirely at the woman's discretion.

Wedding Presents

These are, of course, gifts to both of you. The best guide for distributing these gifts after a divorce is to pay attention to their original provenance. If they emanate from the husband's side of the family, then he has first refusal, and vice versa.

Heirlooms

In general inherited possessions (paintings, furniture, silverware, antiques etc.) will go back to the side of the family from which they originated.

Presents

Within reason, whatever presents you gave each other during your married life are yours to keep. Even if they were extravagantly generous (a car or expensive item of jewellery for example) you should try and respect the original spirit in which they were given.

Now Make an Inventory

Make a list of everything you own (excluding personal possessions and items you have been given individually as gifts). Decide which items you feel you absolutely must have, things you feel you can easily do without, and items over which you're ready to negotiate. Make these decisions when you're on your own and feeling calm and they're more likely to reflect your real desires, rather than an entrenched and obstinate unwillingness to concede anything.

Use the inventory as a basis for negotiations with your ex-partner. It might help if you both ask a friend or relative to help with the negotiations. If the situation gets heated, you may have to go to a mediation service that is trained to help you reach these decisions.

> *"Everybody needs his memories. They keep the wolf of insignificance from the door."*
> Saul Bellow

The Extended Family

"The family – that dear octopus from whose tentacles we never quite escape, nor, in our inmost hearts, ever quite wish to."

Dodie Smith

Post-divorce shock waves will inevitably reverberate throughout your family and extended social circle. If you are lucky, friends and family will be supportive and accepting. They will resist displays of rage on your behalf, and will reassure you of their loyalty without being fiercely partisan. They will never indulge in patronising displays of 'I told you so' sympathy.

Family loyalties generally mean that families stand staunchly by their own members, though not invariably. But while it is tempting to crawl back into the accepting arms of your own family in the raw aftermath of a divorce, it is sensible to resist the temptation to repudiate your in-laws, especially if there are children involved.

Continuing Contact

Now, more than ever, is a time when children need to be able to look out of the (inevitably troubled) immediate family circle for love and support. So it is important that they maintain their relationship with their grandparents, aunts and uncles. You may find that, at the outset, it helps if you sit down and write a letter in which you set out your hopes for their continuing relationship with your children, and your desire to maintain civilised contact with your in-laws despite the trauma of the divorce. Even if children are not involved, you may want to retain contact.

Now is not the time to reiterate grievances or let off steam. Your future relationship with your in-laws may involve a great deal of sweeping unpleasantness under the carpet. But you must remind yourself that this is primarily

** *Allow your children to make direct, unsupervised, contact with grandparents. Give them the phone number or programme it into their mobile phones. It's important for children to feel they've got recourse to grown-ups who are at one remove from the divorce.*

for your children's sake, and they can only benefit from a continuing relationship.

Be vigiliant; you may find that inappropriate remarks are being made about you or your marriage when children are visiting. In-laws might not even realise that they're being tactless, but it is vital that you act fast and put a stop to this. Make a phone call, or – even better – write a considered note, explaining why you are distressed.

New Routines and Rituals

Children love routine, so you might find that a regular date in your diary – tea with Grandma every other Sunday – is the best way of maintaining continuing contact.

If you feel able to do so, invite your in-laws to your home. Your children will appreciate the fact that these relations still occupy a secure place within the family circle. And being the host/hostess will give you back some of the initiative and self-reliance that you may feel has completely deserted you in the immediate aftermath of the divorce.

Greater Involvement

Reach out to your in-laws by keeping them up to date with news of your children. Send them photographs, tell them about school reports, sports prowess, progress with a musical instrument. Remind them about birthdays and liaise with them about presents.

Allow your in-laws to enjoy time alone with your children, and accept that invariably there will be occasions when you feel excluded. These feelings are easier to bear if you picture your children, happy and secure within a family environment.

"It's one of nature's ways that we often feel closer to distant generations than to the generation immediately preceding us."
Igor Stravinsky

The Wider Circle

*"Constant use will
not wear ragged
the fabric of
friendship."*
Dorothy Parker

Inevitably, you will have to accept that, post-divorce, there will be a realignment of loyalties amongst your friends, and your emotional drama will be the subject of much dissection within your social circle.

Many people will have a marked predisposition towards one partner or the other (perhaps because their friendship pre-dates your relationship), and there are bound to be some friendships that are lost while others are consolidated. Friends that you bonded with as a couple might disappear altogether.

This will feel disruptive and disturbing, but wait patiently until the dust settles, and you will find out precisely who your true friends are.

Being Discreet

Your marriage break-up will undoubtedly be the subject of gossip amongst your friends. You can minimise the impact of this gossip by being very circumspect. Only confide in friends whom you trust absolutely, and be very careful about revealing the intimate details of your married life to people who enjoy intrigue and gossip, even though their warmth and sympathy may be very tempting. Be vigilant about using gossip as a means of communicating with your ex-partner – you will find your revelations, like Chinese whispers, become distorted as they are disseminated, exacerbating an already fraught situation. If possible, keep your most private insights and confidences for a professional counsellor, who stands safely outside your social circle.

** Some of your friends will have forged independent relationships with your children or may even be their godparents. Do all you can to facilitate these relationships. An adult who stands outside the family circle may turn into an invaluable support and refuge for your children in the years ahead.

Negotiating Social Minefields

Some people will resist being placed securely in either camp and will want to maintain good relations with both of you. This is laudable, though try to avoid falling into the trap of eliciting (or being forced to listen to) confidences about your ex-partner from a so-called 'neutral' third party.

It's probably best to set out some ground rules at the outset, explaining that you find it hard to see your ex-partner socially, or reassuring friends that it isn't a problem.

When non-aligned friends are hosting major social events they may want to invite both of you. It is important, if they do so, that they explain to each of you that you have both been invited. They should apply no pressure on you to attend, especially if you've made it clear that it's something you can't handle.

If you're refusing an invitation on these grounds, write a little note or email explaining that you're still not ready to socialise with your ex-partner, but expressing your gratitude for the invitation nonetheless.

If you have not been forewarned, and are shocked to find your ex at a social event, retain your dignity. It will just cause embarrassment to host and onlookers alike if you make a scene. If you really do find it intolerable, leave quietly. But tell your host – as temperately as possible – that you would appreciate being told in the future.

DON'T BE A DIVORCE BORE

⇆ You may well be overwhelmed by disillusion, anger, blame and resentment, and the simple truth is that these emotions are extremely disruptive and distressing when displayed to children, family and friends. Many people socialise at a fairly superficial level and find sudden revelations of profound and destructive emotions highly embarrassing. So resist confiding primal emotions to mere acquaintances.

⇆ Entrust your feelings of anger and bitterness to a small circle of friends and confidantes.

⇆ Even though it is an immense effort, exercise self-control when out in public, be calm and non-committal about your feelings, and never speak negatively about your ex.

⇆ Remember, long tales about legal battles, dastardly financial dealings and flaming rows will soon have you struck off the dinner-party guest list, unless told with humour and self-deprecation.

Special Occasions

The impact of a divorce on family and friends is truly tested during the annual round of social milestones – Christmas, birthdays, anniversaries. Negotiation, communication and compromise will help everyone to navigate through the social pitfalls.

Christmas

This is probably the most challenging social hurdle. The relentless promotion of Christmas as a time of family togetherness, peace and goodwill can be very hard when you feel your own family has fractured.

Even if you can't spend the actual day with the kids, you can always celebrate on another day (for example Christmas Eve or Boxing Day). Try not to dwell on what you've lost; now is the time to create new rituals.

Defuse any fall-out amongst your family and friends by being relentlessly polite and civilised. Send friendly Christmas cards to your in-laws and to estranged friends. Remain up-beat and positive throughout the festivities, even if you're finding all the bonhomie very hard-going. At the very least, people will applaud your good manners.

Tips for the Festive Season

⇆ If you are attempting to achieve equitable arrangements over childcare, it's grossly unfair to hog the magic of Christmas with children year after year. Arrange to alternate – at least for Christmas day itself.

⇆ Explain arrangements to the children. Tell them that you (or your ex-partner) will miss them on the actual day, but reassure them that you will make time in which to celebrate.

⇆ Grandparents and extended family will want to see the children as well. Accept that, inevitably, there will be a lot of running around, and don't complain about it.

⇆ If you're the one that's left behind, don't wallow in loneliness and self-pity. Make arrangements; a day with old friends, time with the rest of your family, a holiday.

⇆ Communicate with your ex-partner about presents. You will need to keep a lid on competitive giving, and remember that applies to in-laws as well.

"Life cannot subsist in society but by reciprocal concessions."
Samuel Johnson

** Latest Parentline Plus statistics show that during Christmas 2009, 57% of all calls to the charity's helpline were made from families who had split up or were going through a divorce process.

Birthdays

Continue to send birthday cards to your ex-partner and to your in-laws, and nobody will be able to fault your good manners. Even more importantly, ensure that your children do so. You may feel that these particular dates have ceased to be of any relevance to you, but you must recognise that it's vital that the children recognise them. Help your kids to choose cards and buy presents for their grandparents or for your ex-partner.

When it's time for your children's birthdays, you will need to embark on another round of negotiations. Naturally both parents will want to see their children on, or very near, their birthdays, and it might be that both of you are, separately, giving the children treats – a trip to the cinema, a meal out, a day at the zoo with friends.

If you want your child to have a birthday party, discuss this with your ex-partner. Just one of you should take responsibility for the party (you could offer to do this on alternate years) and make the appropriate arrangements. Your children will find it confusing, and possibly distressing, if they're offered 'competing' parties.

As always, negotiate with your partner about presents and, if possible, set a spending limit. These negotiations might also have to be extended to in-laws, who may not be immune to competition.

Anniversaries

The year will inevitably be littered with significant dates for you and your ex-partner, not least your wedding anniversary.

It may be that this date carries little emotional resonance. If, on the other hand, the date conjures up memories of lavish dinners, beautiful gifts, romantic weekends in Rome or Paris, you should be well-prepared. Don't allow yourself to sink into a morass of gloom on, or near, the date. Pre-empt this possibility by making alternative arrangements – hosting a dinner party, spending time with friends, taking the kids out for a treat.

Significant dates will eventually lose their power. The important thing is not to impose any emotional fall-out on other people, least of all your children.

Rites of Passage

Major rites of passage can pose an etiquette dilemma for divorced couples, their family and friends. While there are few social strictures nowadays relating to the rituals surrounding births and deaths, it is important to exercise discretion, and ensure that your behaviour does not cause offence.

Naming Ceremonies

If you have managed to maintain civilised relations with your partner during the divorce proceedings, you might find yourself invited to the christening/naming ceremony of his/her baby with a new partner. The children from the first marriage may be invited and you may be included in this family celebration.

If you receive an invitation, forensically examine your own feelings about the new baby. If you see this new child as an interloper, liable to supplant your own children, you are nursing feelings of animosity and bitterness that you could find yourself powerless to conceal on the big day.

It might be best to politely refuse the invitation – simply write a short note, thanking the hosts for their kind invitation, and explaining that unfortunately you are unable to attend. You don't need to give a detailed explanation. If you want to mitigate the impact of your non-attendance you can always send a small gift.

Even if you can't face the prospect of the ceremony, accept that your children may be very excited about their new half-sibling, and do everything you can to ensure that they are able to participate.

If you decide to go, take a back seat and don't upstage the parents. Behave impeccably, admire the baby extravagantly, and don't get drunk and embittered.

Children's Milestones

As your children grow up, they will inevitably undergo a number of rites of passage – both religious and secular. These may include confirmation, bar/bat mitzvah, school leaving, graduation. Whatever the occasion, you must remember that these events are central to your child's life, and it is therefore imperative that you put your own bitterness behind you. Your child will want you to attend, and will not want his/her big day to be marred by parental antics.

If the whole day is going to be a painful ordeal, take practical steps. Ask a close friend or a family member to come with you and keep them by your side, with strict instructions to monitor your behaviour, alcohol intake and emotions. With help and support, you should be able to make it through the day with dignity. You may feel that your family has fractured but remember that, for your child, family bonds are indissoluble.

"Good manners and soft words have brought many a difficult thing to pass."
Sir John Vanbrugh

** Divorces don't necessarily terminate relationships with the ex's family. Many people find that their quarrel is with their ex-partner only; they feel nothing but affection for their ex's parents, siblings and so on and may well continue to see them regularly.

Family Funerals

If you have kept on good terms with your ex-partner's extended family, it is only natural to want to attend the funerals of former in-laws You should, of course, check that the family are happy for you to attend first.

But beware, no matter how warmly you feel towards your former family, you are no longer officially part of it. You should not, therefore, head for the family pews at the front, or walk behind the coffin at the end of the service.

If you are accompanying your small child – perhaps to your ex father-in-law's funeral – your relationship to the deceased's grandchild may entitle you to 'family status'. Discreetly ask a family member where you should sit.

Finally, never upstage the blood family when it comes to displays of grief. Maintain a tactful and dignified distance and people will understand that you have come to pay your respects, and appreciate your discretion.

If your ex-partner has died and not remarried, put the travails of the past behind you – your children will need all your support.

If your ex-partner has remarried and subsequently died you may find yourself and your marriage airbrushed out of the eulogies. You may even find yourself completely excluded by a new partner. Don't turn up at the funeral uninvited; instead, think about holding a memorial service with your children's participation.

Symbolic Gestures

"Every beginning is a consequence –
every beginning ends something."

Paul Valéry

Once the dust has settled and the legal practicalities have been negotiated, you may want to turn your attention to more emotionally resonant matters.

Name Changes

Frequently when the name is all that is left of the marriage, newly divorced women are anxious to divest themselves of these last painful vestiges, and decide to revert to their maiden name.

If no children are involved, this is a relatively straightforward decision. You can revert to your maiden name, or even choose a completely new name, which you might see as symbolic of your new life. It is sometimes possible to revert to a maiden name by simply presenting a marriage certificate and decree absolute certificate, but banks and building

societies are more stringent and you may need a Deed Poll to change your name. This is a quick and simple process, requiring no more than an application to the UK Deed Poll Service (you can make an application online at www.ukdps.co.uk). You will receive a personalised Deed Poll document, which you then sign in the presence of a witness. This document is universally recognised.

Think carefully if children are involved. They have grown up with one name, and one identity, and the chances are they will be keen to retain their family name. If you change your name, you will find yourself with a different surname. This is perfectly manageable, but be aware that you will have to repeatedly explain (to schools, doctors, dentists etc.) that you are divorced and have reverted to your maiden name.

It is common for married people to appoint each other as Executors and leave everything to the survivor. If you have one of these wills it is extremely important that the will is revised upon divorce.

** If you are reverting to your maiden name and your children are keeping their father's name, write an explanatory note to the school. This is a common situation, which the school will accommodate, but a note may prevent painful mix-ups.

Some people choose to compromise by creating a double-barrelled name (maiden name-family name, or vice versa). If you do choose to do this, you should discuss it with your children first (if they're old enough) and ensure that this is acceptable to them. Changing children's names will have to be done by Deed Poll, and you will need the consent of everyone with parental responsibility, so you will need the full cooperation of your former partner.

Many women also prefer to be known as Ms after a divorce, finding the title Mrs a painful reminder of a failed marriage.

Spreading the Word

If anyone may be personally affected by your decision to change your name (your ex-in laws, for example), try and tell them face-to-face, or at least send them a handwritten note It is probably easier to inform all your other friends and family by a short and businesslike email (or circular letter).

Making a New Will

You should draw a line under your marriage by making a new will that addresses your changed financial and social status. This is very important if you embark on a new relationship, as you may end up bequeathing a poisoned chalice – a battle over your estate between your 'first' and 'second' family.

WEDDING RINGS

Many people have no desire to carry on wearing a ring after a marriage has imploded. Unlike engagement rings, wedding rings are not treated as outright gifts, so you may want to consider the following options:

⇆ Give the ring back to your ex-partner. At least it won't lurk in your dressing table drawer reminding you of an unhappy chapter in your life. If the ring is a family heirloom, you should certainly give it back to your ex-partner.

⇆ Save the ring for your daughter (or son). It may seem to be a symbol of failure for you, but for your child it represents family bonds, and they may not want to see it lightly abandoned.

⇆ Recycle the ring and have it incorporated into a new piece of jewellery.

⇆ Reappropriate the ring. It is perfectly acceptable to wear your wedding ring on a different finger, on a different hand, or on a chain around your neck.

"What's in a name? That which we call a rose By any other name would smell as sweet."
William Shakespeare

First Steps

The dust has settled and you're finally ready to move on. The emotional after-shock of a divorce can leave you feeling raw and vulnerable. Counselling will help you to feel better about yourself, so you are ready to make a fresh start.

Makeovers

For some newly divorced people, starting again is about literally re-moulding themselves, and they embark on diets and

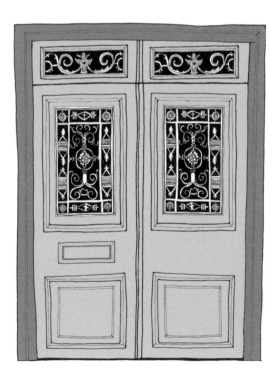

exercise programmes to recapture a svelte pre-marriage figure.

An easier, more indulgent, option is retail therapy. You may find it very heartening to discard the drearier items from your wardrobe and embark on creating a new look. This is the time to put your ex-spouse's likes and dislikes behind you – now you are dressing to please yourself. You must also be aware that your new look is about cutting a dash in the social, and eventually romantic, sphere.

Alternatively you might find yourself transformed by a new haircut, or enjoy being revitalised by a day at a spa.

Indulgences

You have been through an immensely difficult process and now is the time to treat yourself. Sit down and re-evaluate the things that actually give you pleasure – all too often your life will have been moulded by your ex-partner's tastes, and you may have been missing out on your own private passions. If, for example, your idea of heaven is a long country walk or an afternoon movie – and these activities were entirely eschewed by your ex-partner – you can begin to re-discover your chosen recreations.

Treat yourself. Buy an extra good bottle of wine, say yes when a friend suggests a night out. Visit new countries, indulge in sybaritic holidays and broaden your horizons.

** In 1999 108,488 marriages were remarriages for one or both parties. By 2009 this figure had dropped to 80,890 marriages that were remarriages for one or both parties.

Starting Again

You will know you have finally moved on when you find your own misery boring. Then the relationship has truly ended – for both of you – and you can begin to contemplate life after divorce.

If you feel ready to start again, let your friends know. They may well have been waiting in the wings, with potential partners already lined up. But if you do allow yourself to be matched, don't then get huffy when

things don't work out. It's no good saying, "Why did you set me up with someone who didn't call?" when someone was good enough to look out for you in the first place.

If matchmaking doesn't succeed, don't despair… starting over is a long process, so be patient – if friends' contacts fail you, there are hundreds of matchmaking services online, just waiting to unite you with your perfect mate. If you find this prospect daunting, ask a good friend to draft your profile and help you look over possible suitors' replies.

Don't be a Dating Bore

⇆ Resist the temptation to re-live the low points of your marriage with a sympathetic and attentive new partner.

⇆ Beware… detailed tales of communication breakdown, neglect, abuse and infidelity may set alarm bells ringing, and the failure of your marriage may return to haunt you.

⇆ Don't present yourself as an unwitting victim of your ex-partner; your attempts to exculpate yourself will merely look like an inability to face up to reality.

⇆ Always remember that this is a new beginning, a clean slate. Every relationship has its own unique dynamic, and you have to be willing to discard feelings of negativity.

"Turn your wounds into wisdom."
Oprah Winfrey

Dating After A Divorce

Going on your first dates after a divorce can be a challenging experience – you may well feel bruised, rusty and under-confident, but keep trying and you will eventually find someone who gives you a new sense of optimism.

Think about these next steps

⇆ Enjoy the romance
You may be feeling jaded but put bad memories behind you and let yourself go…

⇆ Take it slowly
Repeated introductions of an ever-changing cast of 'new men' and 'new women' in your life can become embarrassing and futile. Give it time.

⇆ Spread the word
When you're sure it's going somewhere, tell important people face-to-face, or drop them a note or an email, explaining that you and your new partner are now an item.

⇆ Clear up any ambiguities
Don't make assumptions and turn up, unannounced, at social occasions with a new man/woman on your arm. Don't leave people guessing, introducing new partners as 'friends'. Clarify the nature of the relationship from the outset. You don't want to turn – yet again – into gossip fodder.

⇆ Be prepared for close scrutiny
Friends and family will feel very protective of you, and may be unusually suspicious of new lovers – especially if there is an alarming age discrepancy. It may feel oppressive, but they really do have your best interests at heart.

⇆ Don't lose your head
Your friends have seen you go through hell, and will be delighted that you have found someone with whom you can start again. But their pleasure will turn to embarrassment and dismay if you go into 'head over heels' mode. People will get very nervous if they feel you haven't learnt anything (at the very least, caution) from your first, failed, marriage.

⇆ Stay discreet
Don't ricochet (publicly at least) from the depths of despair to ecstatic joy. In private, you may feel an absolute conviction that this new relationship is the one, but in public you should play the 'older and wiser' card.

⇆ Spend quality time with the children
You need to integrate them into your dating life, so they don't feel left out or rejected, but you shouldn't attempt to do this until you're confident of the relationship's future. Get your new partner used to spending quality time with your children – this will help greatly if you're contemplating moving in together.

> Divorce rates for the over 50s have soared by 19% to 23,000 a year since 1998, whilst the overall divorce rate has actually fallen 16% to 130,000 a year.

** *Professor Stephen Jenkins, a director of the Institute for Social and Economic Research, has found that, when a man leaves a childless marriage, his income immediately rises by 25%. Women, however, suffer a sharp fall in income.*

"The meeting of two personalities is like the contact of two chemical substances; if there is any reaction, both are transformed."

Carl Gustav Jung

DATING WITH KIDS

Do

⇆ Warn your date that you're bringing your kids: no unexpected surprises.

⇆ If you're bringing children, choose something they'd like to do, e.g. a family movie and pasta lunch, and make them feel that this is a day out for everyone.

⇆ Ensure that your date spends time with your children: send them off to buy ice creams, or let them walk ahead together. That way, they'll get to know each other.

Don't

⇆ Choosing adult activities, regardless of your children's taste, patience, endurance (art galleries, theatres, shopping) will only lead to trouble.

⇆ Be wary of over-compensating for the fact that you'd rather be alone with your date by spoiling your children with sweets, ice-creams, presents etc.

⇆ It's not fair to your kids to make them feel like gooseberries.

New Relationships

If you are lucky enough to find yourself in a new relationship, you must face the challenge of integrating your new partner fully into your life.

Your friends and relations – especially if they were shocked and incredulous at the break-up of your marriage – may find a new partner hard to accept. You cannot control their reactions, but you can ensure that there is no ambiguity about the role of your new partner.

Ex-Partner

Tell your ex that you have found a new partner as soon as possible. It is very painful to hear this news – possibly somewhat garbled – from the children. It may be a very difficult conversation, but it's best to take the bull by the horns.

Anticipate forensic cross-examination from your ex, and don't be defensive about it. It's only natural for estranged parents to be concerned about a new quasi-parent entering their children's lives.

Family

You may have to get used to the fact that your in-laws will never really accept your new partner, and will tolerate him/her at best.

It may help if you write them a short note explaining the importance of this new relationship, reassuring them that you understand how difficult it is, and assuring them that you will do your utmost to remain on civilised terms with them. If children are involved, in-laws will be anxious for your guarantee that a new relationship will not impede their access to the children.

Of the 880,000 stepfamilies in the UK – around one in ten of all families with children – 690,000 have offspring living at home.

** 86 per cent of all stepfamilies have stepchildren from the woman's previous relationship only, 11 per cent have stepchildren from the man's previous relationship only and 3 per cent have children from both parents' previous relationships.

Friends

You shouldn't really have to justify yourself to your friends, but any hesitancy around your new partner is an understandable, protective reaction. If they're used to seeing you with your ex, then a new partner will take some getting used to.

Take it slowly, don't assume your new partner is inevitably invited. Check before any social event to ensure if he/she is welcome – some friends may, after all, be suffering from divided loyalties, and feel that friendliness towards your new partner is a betrayal of their friendship with your ex.

If you feel that your new partner is consistently excluded, sit down and discuss it openly with your friends, or if this is uncomfortable, write a brief non-confrontational note. If they understand how important it is to you, they may be able to move towards a more welcoming attitude.

Helping Children Understand

The hardest thing of all is introducing a new partner into your children's life. Your children may secretly have been plotting (or at least fantasising about) your reunion with your ex, and a new partner is a stark confirmation that their parents' marriage is truly over.

Resistance is inevitable, but follow these simple rules to make the transition as civilised as possible:

⇆ Take if slowly. Suddenly finding a 'new daddy/mummy' sitting at the breakfast table will shock most children to the core. Initially, restrict overnight stays to the times when your children are staying with your ex.

⇆ Gradually introduce your children to your partner by involving them in activities together – day trips out, meals together, trips to the cinema.

⇆ Explain at this stage that, while your new partner is very important to you, he/she will never replace their real mum or dad.

⇆ Never let your new partner distract you from your children; they must not be made to feel that your love for them has diminished in any way.

⇆ Resist public intimacy. Unless your children are tiny, and therefore oblivious, it will make them feel very excluded.

⇆ Be discreet about bedroom activities, and ensure that you're not taken by surprise.

⇆ Be patient. Your children will naturally feel that bonding with a new partner is disloyal to their real parent, and it will take time for them to understand that your new relationship may be a positive development in their lives.

"Love is the greatest refreshment in life."
Pablo Picasso

Divorce and Weddings

"Marriage is a great institution,
but I'm not ready for an institution."

Mae West

Weddings are major social occasions, and there is often a huge emotional investment in their success. Whether you or your partner are marrying again, or watching your own children tie the knot, the carapace of good manners can armour you against destructive feelings of rage and powerlessness.

Attending your Ex-Partner's Wedding

Traditionally ex-partners weren't invited to remarriages, but social customs have become more fluid, and you may find yourself on the guest list. If the whole notion of the remarriage makes you feel ill, politely refuse the invitation (no explanation needed).

If you do attend your ex-partner's wedding it is imperative that you act impeccably.

Don't attempt to upstage the bride or groom. Don't drink too much and turn maudlin or aggressive. You might be wise to tip off friends to look out for you, and make it their job to escort you home as soon as they see your social façade begin to wobble.

The bride or groom may want children from previous marriages to play an important role on the big day, e.g. act as pages or bridesmaids. Accept that this is their right and do everything you can to facilitate your children's participation. Never threaten your ex-partner with non-cooperation.

Remarriages

The time may come when you are contemplating tying the knot once again. If you're planning to take this big step follow these simple rules:

In 2007 the average age for men remarrying was 46.5, while the average age for women was 43.5.

** 35% of all weddings in the UK are second or subsequent marriages.

⇆ Don't allow yourself to become jaded. While the trappings of the wedding may bring back unhappy memories, your new partner may be marrying for the first time, and will be enthusiastic to embark on a new adventure.

⇆ Participate fully and do not allow the failure of your first marriage to poison the second wedding day.

⇆ Be prepared to find an air of awkwardness and nervousness permeating relations with your new in-laws. This is quite understandable – you do not have a good track record. Devote all your energies to reassuring them of your commitment to the new marriage.

⇆ Don't sweep your first marriage under the carpet as it may cause confusion for your children and extended family.

⇆ It is quite appropriate to make a brief reference to a previous marriage in the speeches – keep any allusions wry, affectionate and light-hearted.

⇆ Behave as if you are embracing your past, not obliterating it.

Children's Weddings

If you are hosting or attending the wedding of one of your children from a previous marriage, remember that it is your son's or daughter's big day. Whatever their wishes, you must accede. Behave in a civilised manner, without a hint of bitterness.

If there is abiding antagonism between you and your ex-partner, make some simple provisions. Plan the seating carefully to avoid conflict between the different 'sides', but close enough to appear unified.

Split wedding duties. For example, the natural father could walk the bride down the aisle and the stepfather could give a speech. At the reception you could opt for three 'top' tables. Each of the separated parents can host their own table, leaving the bride and groom to sit with bridesmaids, ushers and friends.

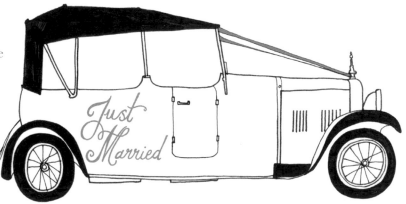

Correct Forms of Address

While a man's style of address post-divorce does not change, divorced women can opt for one of a number of name choices, and addressing them can be an etiquette minefield. If you're a newly divorced woman, and sensitive about how you're addressed, you must be prepared to send out a notification to friends, family, businesses. Inevitably, there will be mistakes, so it's best if you can resign yourself to this and accept *faux-pas* with good grace.

Traditional Address

By convention a divorcee would adopt the style of, for example, Mrs Caroline Smith (i.e. retaining her title of 'Mrs' and her married surname 'Smith', but using her own forename, i.e. no longer 'Mrs John Smith').

Contemporary Address

This rule may still be followed by some older women, but it is by no means the norm for younger women. Many women, especially those who combine a working life with a married life, choose not to use their husband's surname at all. If a woman has retained her maiden name throughout the marriage her only decision, on becoming divorced, is whether she prefers to be Mrs, Miss or Ms Janie Jones, for example, or just Janie Jones with no title.

Divorcing women who have assumed their husband's surname may revert to their maiden name. This happens most often where there are no children from the marriage.

If there are children, however, women may choose to retain their married surnames, and continue to use 'Mrs', just in order to maintain the status quo and to avoid a situation where the mother is using a different surname to that of her children.

Play it Safe

People may well settle on the conventional option – 'Mrs Caroline Smith' (i.e. they will use the forename and the married surname). Don't be offended if this does not reflect your chosen form of address – simply write a polite note saying that from now on you're using the following. e.g. Ms Caroline Jones.

Women with Titles

When a peeress (i.e. a duchess, marchioness, countess, viscountess or baroness) obtains a divorce, the general rule is that she places her forename before her title, for example, Mary, Duchess of Hampshire. This is purely a practical measure to avoid confusion should the peer in question marry again.

In the event of a divorced peer remaining unmarried there is no reason why his former wife should not continue to use her title without the qualification of her forename.

"If names are not correct, language will not be in accordance with the truth of things"
Confucius

** More than 90,000 people used two leading online services to change their name by Deed Poll in 2010, an increase of more than 30% on 2009. The increase has mostly been divorced women reverting to their maiden names or changing their children's surnames to fit in with their new family.

Wording Invitations

Everyone wants to get formal invitations right, especially wedding invitations. The vicissitudes of family life – divorces, remarriages, step-parents – can all be accommodated on formal invitations if you follow the wording set out below:

If the bride's mother is the hostess:

> Mrs John Robinson
> requests the pleasure of
> your company at the marriage
> of her daughter
> Caroline

If the bride's father is the host:

> Mr John Robinson
> requests the pleasure of
> your company at the marriage
> of his daughter
> Caroline

If the bride's mother and stepfather are the joint host/ hostess:

> Mr and Mrs Edgar Forsythe
> request the pleasure of
> your company at the marriage
> of her daughter
> Caroline Robinson

If the bride's father and her stepmother are the joint host/hostess:

> Mr and Mrs John Robinson
> request the pleasure of
> your company at the marriage
> of his daughter
> Caroline

Where the bride's stepmother is the hostess:

> Mrs John Robinson
> requests the pleasure of
> your company at the marriage
> of her stepdaughter
> Caroline

If the bride's parents are divorced, but are co-hosting the wedding:

> Mr John Robinson and Mrs Edgar Forsythe*
> request the pleasure of
> your company at the marriage
> of their daughter
> Caroline

* 'Mrs Jane Robinson' if she has not remarried and has kept her married name.

If the bride is divorced and still using her married name, she is described as 'Mrs Jane (married name)'. If she has reverted to her maiden name, only her forename is listed.

The Process of Divorce

"Next to a battle lost, the greatest misery is a battle won."

Duke of Wellington

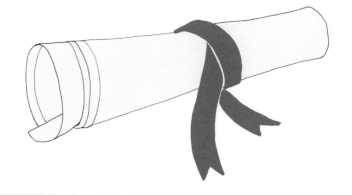

Grounds for Divorce

The only basis for divorce in England is the irretrievable breakdown of a marriage. This can be established by:

• the other party's adultery
• the other party's unreasonable behaviour
• desertion for two years by the other party
• a separation for two years with the other spouse's consent
• separation for five years.

There is no longer a requirement to name a co-Respondent in adultery proceedings.

If possible, any allegations about behaviour, which are usually drafted in a fairly anodyne form, will be agreed by both spouses (or their solicitors) before proceedings begin. Any disagreements about behaviour may lead to the divorce proceedings being defended.

Divorce Proceedings (Undefended)

First step...
The Divorce Application is lodged at Court with a form setting out proposed arrangements for any children. The original marriage certificate (or a certified copy obtained from a Registrar) is also sent to the Court, where it is retained.

The Divorce Application also contains an application for all forms of financial remedy on behalf of the Applicant and any children.

3–4 days later...
The Court issues the Divorce Application, which is served on the other spouse (the Respondent).

* *In 2008, for the fourth consecutive year, both men and women in their late twenties had the highest divorce rates of all five-year age groups with 22.8 divorces per 1,000 married men aged 25 to 29 and 26.0 divorces per 1,000 married women aged 25 to 29.*

---

29 days later...

This is the amount of time allowed to the Respondent in which to confirm they have received the Application, and to state whether they will defend the proceedings. If they are not defending the proceedings, the Respondent signs a statement swearing the contents of the Application are true and returns it to Court. This is a public document.

One month later...

Once the Judge has received the statement a date is set (about a month later) for the first decree of divorce, the decree nisi. The decree nisi is pronounced in open court, though neither party needs attend. Other than that, undefended divorce proceedings are held in private and members of the public do not have access to the Court file.

Six weeks and a day later...

The Applicant can now apply for the decree absolute which dissolves the marriage. It is usual, however, to wait for financial issues to be resolved before applying for the decree absolute. This ensures that spousal benefits under any pensions or life policies are not lost if one party were to die in the meantime.

If the Applicant fails to apply for the decree absolute, the Respondent can make an application after three months have elapsed.

Defended Divorce

If the Respondent decides to defend the proceedings, this will be confirmed after the Application has been issued and there will be a directions appointment, when the Court tries to broker an agreement. If that is unsuccessful, there will be a trial, at which both parties involved, and any witnesses, attend to give evidence. Members of the public may sit in court during the trial.

At this hearing evidence will be given to the judge, who will then have to decide if a divorce should be granted.

In the meantime the Court may need to resolve child care and financial issues.

Child Care Issues

If separating parents are unable to reach an agreement over arrangements for contact with their children or to agree with whom their children will live, the Court may adjudicate. The Court can make joint residence orders so that a child lives for part of the time with each parent, or it may order one parent has a residence order and the other a contact order.

The Court can also make an order on disputed issues such as the school the children should attend, or whether they should be brought up in a particular religious faith.

The Court can be asked to prohibit the taking of a course of action by one parent to which the other parent objects.

Parental Responsibility

This is defined as all the right, duties, powers and responsibilities which by law a parent of a child has in relation to the child and his or her property.

A mother automatically has parental responsibility for her child. A father will also automatically have parental responsibility if he is married to the mother or he is named on the birth certificate.

If the father does not have parental responsibiliy, the mother can grant it to him. If she refuses to do so, the father can make an application to the Court for a Parental Responsibility Order.

Child Care Proceedings

After any of the applications already outlined have been made to the Court, a 'conciliation appointment' is listed to take place about six weeks later.

Conciliation Appointment: this is presided over by a District Judge and a Court Reporting Officer. Both divorcing parties are required to attend this hearing and may be expected to speak.

They may also be directed to go to to a separate room with the Court Reporting Officer to explore issues further before reaching a final agreement.

If this proceeding does not succeed, the Court will make directions setting a timetable for a final hearing. Witness statements and expert evidence may need to be compiled. A Court Reporting Officer will be required to interview both parties and (if old enough) any children involved and make a report.

The final hearing: this usually takes place five to eight months after the Conciliation Appointment if no agreement has already been reached. The hearing takes place in private; members of the public and press have no access to the hearings or documents.

At the end of the proceedings the Court makes its order. It is unusual for there to be an award of costs in hearings of this type – usually both parties pay their own costs.

> One in five men and women divorcing in 2008 had a previous marriage ending in divorce. This proportion has almost doubled since 1981

** For 67 per cent of divorces in 2008, the wife was granted the divorce. For all divorces granted to an individual (rather than jointly to both), behaviour was the most common reason for divorce.

Financial Issues

When a negotiated settlement is not reached Court proceedings may be necessary.

The First Appointment

This usually takes place 14 to 18 weeks after an application for financial remedy (Form A) has been issued. There is a strict timetable:

Five weeks before First Appointment

Each party swears a sworn statement (Form E), on which disclosure is made. Supporting documents, such as bank statements, accounts, salary advice, are provided.

Two weeks before First Appointment

Each party serves on the other a statement of the issues in the case, a chronology and a questionnaire – both parties may seek further information/documents arising from the other's Form E.

The First Appointment

The District Judge will decide on the further orders necessary to progress the case. For example, if there is disagreement over assets he may order a professional valuation.

The FDR

This usually takes place three to five months after the First Appointment.

During this time, both parties have a positive duty to negotiate, and comply with the Court's directions. Most cases settle at, or shortly after, the FDR.

If settlement is not agreed, the Judge will give the necessary directions to prepare the case for trial. Both parties will be required to set out their case in sworn statements.

The Final Hearing

This hearing usually takes place six to eight months after the FDR, and lasts between two and five days.

After hearing oral evidence from both sides, as well as witnesses and experts, the Judge will give judgment and make a final order (sometimes after a delay of some weeks).

At this stage, any arguments about costs and who is to pay them may be heard.

Frequently Asked Questions

How long will this process take?
This will depend on the extent to which any children's and financial issues can be agreed. Divorce and associated proceedings can be as swift or as drawn out as the parties decide. If both want a fair and quick conclusion then it should not take too long. If one, or both, are intransigent then court proceedings may well be inevitable and lengthy. Bitterly contested proceedings are not only emotionally draining for the adults they will affect the children of the relationship, who also have to deal with the uncertainty that hangs over their family life.

What will happen to the family home?
Depending on the family's circumstances, the home will either be transferred to one of the couple or sold. If the family home has to be sold, don't panic. Home is where your family is, and often a new start in life deserves a new home too.

My spouse was having an affair. Will she/he be penalised?
Adultery is not penalised by the courts. Only rarely will conduct be taken into account by the courts when dividing marital assets. Likewise, marital conduct rarely has an impact on child care arrangements; rather the court will consider a variety of issues when determining future child care arrangements.

I'm the one who wants a divorce. Will I lose my half of the house?
Neither the cause of the breakdown of the marriage nor which party issues proceedings has any bearing on the division of assets or children's issues.

Should I still be using our joint account?
If you are the payer, you might want to think about curtailing the expenditure on the joint account. If you are the payee, maintain the status quo until being informed otherwise.

Does divorce have to be adversarial?
No. Separation is difficult and painful but it is possible to minimise its effects by taking an amicable and conciliatory approach.

Will I have to go to court?
If all other forms of communication break down and there is little agreement between you, going to court is a likely outcome, but it should not be the first move. Mediation and counselling are both sensible options, as is talking to your partner (with the help of lawyers if necessary) in order to come to a fair and swift conclusion.

Is this process going to be costly?
The overall legal cost will depend entirely on the extent of disagreement between you and

your spouse. A long, drawn out dispute can be very expensive. The alternative – thorough, sensible negotiation – does not have to cost the earth.

How can I shelter my children from all this nastiness?

Children can become emotionally affected if they are exposed to a highly charged parental dispute. Listen to your children, they may be more insightful than you think. Reassure them that no matter what the outcome, both parents will be there for love and support.

How much, if any, contact should I have with my ex-partner?

No matter how difficult it may be, if you can keep lines of communication open then you should try to do so and maintain a dialogue with your spouse.

What about the family pet?

A family pet will often be cherished and can become the source of argument. Be mature and discuss this with your ex-partner. Often it is sensible for the pet to stay with the parent with primary care of the children.

Should I stay in touch with in-laws?

It is important to retain good familial ties during and following separation. Your ex-partner's family are still your children's aunts, uncles, cousins and grandparents. Children will want to stay connected to their extended families.

What happens if I've started dating during proceedings?

It is important to take things slowly during divorce proceedings, and not to disrupt the life of your children too much. A parent moving out of the family home is hard enough; introductions to a new partner should be done sensitively.

If I wish to return overseas to my country of origin, can I take my children with me?

You cannot permanently remove your children from the UK without the prior agreement of your spouse or permission of the court.

Glossary

Access
See Contact.

Acknowledgment of Service
A form which has to be completed, signed and returned to the court where divorce proceedings were issued confirming receipt of the divorce petition.

Affidavit
A written, sworn, statement of evidence.

Ancillary relief / Financial remedy
Discretionary re-distribution by the courts of the property and income of spouses or civil partners upon divorce or dissolution of a marriage.

Civil partnership
The legal status acquired by same-sex couples who formally register their relationship, giving them the same legal rights, obligations and responsibilities as married couples.

CAFCASS
The Children and Family Court Advisory and Support Service.

Chattels
The contents of a house and personal effects.

Conditional Order
The first of the two orders of dissolution of a civil partnership which confirms that the ground for dissolution has been approved by the court.

Contact
Arrangements about parental access to the child.

Contact Order
An order requiring the person with whom the child lives (the residential parent) to allow the child to visit, or stay with, or have other access with the person named in the order.

Consent Order
Any order made by agreement reached between the parties (generally in relation to financial issues but also in relation to care arrangements for children).

Cross-examination
Questioning of a witness by a party other than the party who called the witness.

Decree Absolute of Divorce
The final decree in divorce proceedings, the effect of which is to dissolve the marriage.

Decree Nisi of Divorce
The first of the two decrees of divorce which confirms that the ground for divorce has been approved by the Court.

Disclosure
The provision of information and documents relevant to court proceedings. In the context of financial proceedings and proceedings in relation to children both parties have a duty to give full and frank disclosure. If the duty is breached, a later court order could be set aside.

Dissolution / Civil Partnership Order
The final order which brings a civil partnership to an end.

Divorce / Matrimonial Order
The legal termination of a marriage.

Evidence in chief
The evidence given by a witness for the party who called him or her to testify.

Family Therapy
Family therapy (or 'couple and family therapy', 'family systems therapy') is a branch of psychotherapy that works with families and couples to assist them in coming to terms with the changed dynamic following separation.

Form E
A pro forma document that is used to provide disclosure in financial proceedings.

Injunction
A court order prohibiting a person from doing something or requiring a person to do something.

Judicial Separation
A decree of Judicial Separation brings to an end all marital obligations; it does not however dissolve the marriage.

Marital property agreements
Pre-nuptial agreements, post-nuptial agreements, and separation agreements; collectively known as 'nuptial agreements'.

Mediation
An alternative to litigation for couples who are otherwise unable to reach agreements concerning their children and finances. A mediator assists the couple to discuss and reach agreement on these issues.

Office copy
A copy of an official document, supplied and marked as such by the office that issued the original.

Parental responsibility
Defined as all the rights, duties, powers and responsibilities which by law a parent of a child has in relation to the child and his and her property.

Petition / Application
The form by which proceedings for divorce or dissolution are commenced.

Petitioner / Applicant
The person applying for divorce.

Post-nuptial agreement
An agreement made during marriage or civil partnership which seeks to regulate the couple's financial affairs during the relationship or to determine the division of their property in the event of divorce, dissolution or separation.

Pre-action protocol
Statements of best practice concerning pre-litigation conduct.

Pre-nuptial agreement (or contract)
An agreement made before marriage or civil partnership which seeks to regulate the couple's financial affairs during the relationship or to determine the division of their property in the event of divorce, dissolution or separation. Often referred to colloquially as a 'pre-nup' and in some cases as an 'ante-nuptial agreement'.

Privilege
The right of a party to refuse to disclose a document or produce a document or to refuse to answer questions (a legal obligation in most litigation proceedings) on the ground of some special interest recognised by law.

Prohibited Steps Order
A court order that prohibits certain actions that a parent proposes to take, such as moving out of the country or changing a child's surname.

Respondent

The spouse who is replying to an application for divorce.

Residence Order

An order settling arrangements relating to where the child lives, and with whom. The order is made in relation to one of the parents, and confers parental responsibility on that person (if they did not already have parental responsibility for the child).

Seal

A mark that the court puts on a document to indicate that the court has issued the document.

Separation

The informal termination of the spouses' or civil partners' relationship, when they cease to live in a joint household. Separation may or may not be followed by divorce or dissolution of the partnership.

Separation agreement

An agreement made when a couple are contemplating separation or have already separated, making financial arrangements for a period of separation and subsequent divorce or dissolution.

Service

Legal steps required to bring court documents to a person's attention.

Set aside

An application to cancel a judgment or order or a step taken by a party in the proceedings.

Skeleton argument

A skeleton argument is intended to identify both for the parties and the court those points that are in issue, and the nature of the argument in relation to those points that are in issue. It is not a substitute for oral argument.

Specific Issue Order

A court order that specifies actions to be taken regarding a specific child-related issue, such as where the child will attend school or what religion the child should observe.

Spouse

One of the parties to a marriage or a civil partnership.

Stay

A stay imposes a halt on proceedings, apart from the taking of any steps allowed by the rules or the terms of the stay. Proceedings can be continued if a stay is lifted. Alternatively, a stay may be imposed preventing the enforcement of a court order pending an appeal against the terms of the order that has been stayed.

Strike out

This means the court ordering written material to be deleted so that it may no longer be relied upon. Alternatively it may mean dismissing an application by either party.

Without prejudice

Negotiations with a view to settlement are usually conducted 'without prejudice', which means that the circumstances in which the content of those negotiations may be revealed to the court are very restricted.

Witness statement

A document recording the evidence of a person, which is signed by that person and is accompanied by a statement confirming that the contents of the statement are true.

Useful addresses

Bar Council
The Bar Council represents the interests of barristers. Its role is to promote and improve the services and functions of the Bar.
www.barcouncil.org.uk

Child Support Agency
The CSA ensures that parents who live apart from their children contribute financially to their upkeep by paying child maintenance. The CSA can calculate, set up and administer child maintenance payments.
www.csa.gov.uk

Citizen's Advice Bureau
The CAB can offer help and support after a relationship breakdown. It will help you to find out what your rights are, and will advise you on issues like making a will, registering a birth or changing your name, and where else to go for help.
www.adviceguide.org.uk

Coram
A children's charity that will advise parents on how to support their children through this difficult time.
www.coram.org.uk

Dept. for Work & Pensions
This government website will help you explore the benefits and financial support you may be entitled to after your divorce
www.direct.gov.uk/en/MoneyTaxAndBenefits/index

Institute of Family Therapy
An institute of professional therapists, providing Family Mediation to help couples (with or without children) deal with separation and divorce without embarking on a costly legal process.
www.instituteoffamilytherapy.org.uk

The Law Society
The Law Society represents, protects and promotes solicitors in England and Wales, from negotiating with and lobbying the profession's regulators, government and others, to offering training and advice.
www.lawsociety.org.uk

National Family Mediation
NFM is a network of Family Mediation Services which offers help to those affected by separation and divorce.
www.nfm.org.uk

Relate
Relate offers advice, relationship counselling, sex therapy, workshops, mediation, consultations and support face-to-face, by phone and through this website.
www.relate.org.uk

Resolution
Resolution's 5,500 members are family lawyers committed to the constructive, non-confrontational resolution of family disputes. They encourage solutions that consider the needs of the whole family - and the best interests of children.
www.resolution.org.uk

Reunite
The leading UK charity specialising in international parental child abduction.
www.reunite.org